The Cryptocurrency Bible 2021-2022

Ultimate Guide to Make Money; Maximize Crypto Profits with Investment Tips & Trading Strategies
(Bitcoin, Ethereum, Ripple, Cardano, Chainlink, Dogecoin & Altcoins)

Edition 3.0

STELLAR MOON PUBLISHING

Disclaimer

Cryptotrading in 2021 & 2022

Crypto trading for beginners is becoming more and more popular. You see, every day there are more people who start with crypto trading. And that's not strange, because there is a lot of profit to be made. However, of course you have to do a lot for this. You can't become big with crypto trading without some knowledge. That's why in this book we explain to you exactly what you need to know if you're still a beginner and you want to start with crypto trading.

What is crypto trading?
When you want to invest your money, you can do that in different ways. You can choose to invest it in stocks, or for instance by practicing Forex trading. However, more and more traders choose to invest their money in something else than Forex or stocks. Indeed, investing in cryptocurrency is becoming increasingly popular.

Crypto trading is trading in cryptocurrencies. The goal is to buy a cryptocurrency for a low amount, and then sell it again for a higher amount. Trading cryptocurrency is becoming more popular not only among young people, but also among traders who would normally only invest in stocks.

Before you can successfully crypto trade, it is important to learn how the crypto world works. You can do this by taking a crypto training course, or by reading our tips for beginners. It is important to know that these are of course tips, and we cannot guarantee that you will actually make money with them.

Crypto coins and tokens
There are both crypto coins and tokens. However, there is a big difference between these two concepts. A crypto currency is in fact a coin that runs on its own blockchain. For example, the crypto currency of Ethereum is Ether (ETH), and the crypto currency of the Bitcoin blockchain is Bitcoin (BTC). A blockchain can only represent one crypto currency.

However, multiple tokens can run on a blockchain. A token is something that uses the technology of another blockchain. For example, there are tokens that run on Ethereum's blockchain.

Different crypto currencies
There are different types of crypto currencies. Of course, Bitcoin (BTC) is both the first and the most well-known crypto currency. However, there are many more coins than just Bitcoin, which we call altcoins (alternative coins).

The best known altcoins are Ethereum (ETH), Dogecoin (DOGE), Solana (SOL), Ripple (XRP) and of course Cardano (ADA). When you are a beginner, it is important that you know which cryptocurrency you can trade in. Therefore, do a lot of research on the crypto currencies that are available. On CoinMarketcap you can find all kinds of information such as the price of Bitcoin (BTC) and alt coins.

The latest Bitcoin Crash

It can't have escaped anyone's attention: Bitcoin has taken heavy blows. Like any financial market, Bitcoin trading is led by emotion.

Or rather, the crypto currency investors are led by emotion and Elon Musk's recent tweets are causing a lot of FUD ("Fear, Uncertainty, Doubt"). Completely unexpected, he attacked Bitcoin on fossil fueled energy consumption and carbon footprint.

Despite the fact that this story has been debunked many times, people are very sensitive to this, and when such a big celebrity shouts something, most people believe it immediately and fear gathers around. What does this mean for the Bitcoin price and other crypto currencies?

Stellar Moon Publishing compiled this book to offer an insight into the best trading tips and strategies for 2021. This book has been written by a group of cryptocurrency experts. With this book, we strive to provide you with the best curated information on cryptocurrency trading and investments.

Just as Bitcoin's price was recently rebounding the fear set in and the deflation was significant. The advantage is that the real solid support levels now stand out. In spite of all the panic: the $30,000 barrier appears not to be broken anytime soon. Not even Elon can break it down that far!

And bitcoin made a great recovery after that with a lot of positive news backing it up, we will have a short overview of what that news entails and how it could influence on the future of bitcoin and cryptocurrencies.

More future predictions
Stock market strategist Tom Lee of asset manager Fundstrat continues to believe in the resurrection of bitcoin. In an analysis published Monday, Lee indicated that the major crypto currency could set new records if the stock market takes the lead with a renewed stock market rally.

Lee maintains his forecast that bitcoin could rise to a level of $125,000 this year. On Wednesday, bitcoin quoted a level of $37,000.

In mid-April, bitcoin reached a record level of about $65,000. Then the crypto currency fell back to just above $30,000 in May.

Lee thinks bitcoin is "bottoming out. He deduces this in part from the fact that bitcoin's price hardly reacts to negative news coverage anymore.

In the stock market, stock market indices such as the broad S&P 500 index and the Dow Jones index are hovering against recent record levels. "If the S&P 500 reaches a new all-time high, it is obvious that crypto stocks will also be looking for new records," Lee says.

To this, Lee adds in his analysis that new records for major stock indices do not mean that bitcoin will immediately go to the old record level. A "consolidation" between $35,000 and $60,000 is then initially likely, Lee writes.

"We will see bitcoin rise above $125,000 before the end of the year, but are still somewhat cautious in the short term. Once bitcoin quotes above $40,000, that confirms the contention that the $30,000 level has been the bottom in 2021," Lee concludes.

Twice as much bitcoin investors in 2021
According to Crypto.com, there were 106 million users/owners of crypto currencies at the beginning of this year. This is consistent with earlier research by the University of Cambridge, which estimated the number

of crypto users at 101 million after the third quarter of 2020, up from only 35 million users in 2018.

Over the course of 2021, crypto currencies are gaining substantially in popularity. The number of users has since doubled to 221 million in June, Crypto.com says. According to the platform, different factors did play a role in the first months of the first half of the year than in the second:

In January and February, it was mainly Bitcoin that drove global crypto adoption. Ethereum (ether) is confirmed in the survey as the clear number two, albeit at a considerable distance from Bitcoin.
In the spring, it was mostly altcoins, the alternative smaller coins such as Dogecoin, that took off. As a result, Bitcoin's market share sank from 67 percent in January to another 51 percent at the end of June.
"Likely events that boosted crypto currency acceptance were massive institutional acceptance and increasingly easy crypto currency trading, along with the celebrity effect of Elon Musk," writes Crypto.com.

Table of Contents

Your FREE Book

If you want to make a profitable start in the world of cryptocurrency, make sure to download our free bonus with **12 extremely valuable tips for beginners!**

With this book and these tips, you're guaranteed to make a great start with your future investments!

Sign up here to get instant access and kickstart your crypto success:

https://campsite.bio/stellarmoonpublishing

Our Crypto Expert Trading Course

Are you looking for a new way to invest?

Are you looking to make some money?

Interested in investing but do not know where to start?

Do you want to start your crypto trading with the knowledge of reputable experts in finance and investment?

The crypto Expert Trading Course is the most comprehensive course on trading and investing with cryptocurrencies. You will learn how to trade in just a few minutes per day. We

13

teach you everything from technical analysis, risk management, and much more.

Our goal is to help you become a successful trader so that your financial future can be secure.

Investing has never been easier with our step-by-step blueprint that teaches beginners how to trade like an expert – with the potential of making huge profits!

The best part about this course is taught by experts. So, what are you waiting for? Start today!

For more information, visit this link:

https://payhip.com/b/ork8N

Our books

Check out our other book to learn more about NFTs, NFT trading and selling, how to make profit and essential tips and strategies for a fail-proof start in the NFT universe.

Join the exclusive Stellar Moon Publishing Circle, you'll get instant access to **12 Extremely Valuable Crypto Tips**!

Besides that, you'll also get instant access to our mailing list with updates from our experts every week!

Sign up here today:

https://campsite.bio/stellarmoonpublishing

The Bitcoin future in 2021

Bitcoin rises to $115,000 in August 2021, Pantera expects
Pantera Capital founder and CEO Dan Morehead stands by his incredibly positive forecast for bitcoin in 2021. He claims bitcoin is still well on its way to becoming $115,000 by August of this year.

Stock to flow prediction
In the January version of Pantera's Blockchain mailing, Morehead writes that bitcoin's price movements, although delayed by a week, are proceeding exactly as predicted based on the stock-to-flow forecast published last year.

'Bitcoin is right on track with the forecast we shared in our April mailing. Our analysis was based on comparing the decline in the supply/flow of bitcoin compared to the outstanding stock at the time of each halving, and the subsequent impact on the price.'

Catching up on bitcoin
According to Pantera's predictions, the price of bitcoin was lagging by as much as 15 weeks in July 2020. In December, bitcoin began to catch up with Pantera's predictions and in mid-January, the leading cryptocurrency reached the ninth milestone in Pantera's forecast after climbing to $38,000. If the bitcoin price continues to follow his predictions, the currency will rise to $45,268 on February 15.

Impact of halving
The investment fund's predictions are made based on bitcoin's halving cycle. Morehead says that historically, the bitcoin price always rises after each halving. Halves take place every four years.

After the first halving in 2012, bitcoin supply decreased by just over 15% in a 446-day period, while block rewards were halved from 50 to 25 BTC. Subsequently, the entire world witnessed a 9,212% increase in the bitcoin price. After the halving in 2016, bitcoin rose by 2,910%.

If bitcoin follows Pantera's predicted trajectory, Morehead expects the cryptocurrency to peak in August 2021 with a value of $115,212. That's an increase of more than 1,091% after halving in May 2020.

At stellar moon publishing, we think that a new all-time high for bitcoin is possible this year but highly unlikely that it will happen by the end of august. That's also when this book will probably be released, so we will see if pantera's prediction is true.

Bitcoin ETF fund in Europe?

France's Melanion Capital is the first party in Europe to launch a European-regulated bitcoin ETF. The Paris-based investment fund has received permission from French regulators to launch an ETF that meets the European UCITS standard.

UCITS stands for Undertakings fort he Collective Investment in Transferable Securities and refers to a legal framework built for trading funds on a European level. Funds that meet the UCITS standard are considered the most secure on the continent and are therefore in high demand by investors. Which makes it extra interesting that Melanion is coming out with a bitcoin ETF that meets the UCITS standard.

Fund must track a basket of 30 stocks
It is intended that Melanion's new fund will follow a basket of up to 30 stocks in different sectors that are related to bitcoin. Here you have to think about cryptocurrency miners, but also so-called blockchain companies. Which, according to Melanion, show up to 90 percent correlation with bitcoin and thus largely follow the price of the most dominant cryptocurrency.

"I have yet to see any funds under the UCITS umbrella that focus entirely on digital assets," lawyer Winston Penhall of Keystone Law in London told the Financial Times. How lawmakers view bitcoin and other cryptocurrencies is still unclear in many cases, according to Penhall, he added to his statements.

UCITS funds sold in Europe are also generally popular in Asia and Latin America. Globally, they are seen as the gold standard in terms of regulation for funds. The majority of European funds adhere to the UCITS standard, which offers a high level of protection to investors. However, the standards were created 30 years ago and bitcoin and other cryptocurrencies were obviously not taken into consideration when drafting them.

Rules not yet there to include bitcoin in fund
As a result, most national legislators interpret UCITS rules to mean that digital assets like bitcoin cannot be directly included in a fund. That makes it virtually impossible to launch a UCITS fund that invests primarily in bitcoin. "Most of the gates of traditional finance are closing on bitcoin. The ETF was a huge challenge because of the sensitivities and politics surrounding bitcoin and investing in bitcoin," said Jad Comair, Melanion's CEO.

As a result, Melanion will use the bitcoin ETF to invest primarily in miners such as Argo Blockchain and Riot Blockchain. In addition, investment company Galaxy Digital of Mike Novogratz can expect investments and broker Voyager Digital is also on the list. Stocks are considered based on the sensitivity they show to bitcoin. The higher the correlation, the more likely they are to be included.

There are already several financial products that track the price of bitcoin, such as the Wisdom Bitcoin ETP that you can buy in Europe. Although this is a regulated financial product it does not meet the UCITS standard and cannot put that sought-after label on it. As a result, a lot of capital is unlikely to be able to invest in such investment products because they offer sufficient protection for investors.

Bitcoin in El Salvador and the World Bank

The World Bank has refused to help El Salvador integrate Bitcoin into its financial infrastructure, a report on Reuters said today.

The Central American country made history last week when it passed a bill that made Bitcoin legal tender. Since then, however, various authorities, including the IMF, have given the idea cold water.

With the World Bank also shunning Bitcoin, it is clear that global governments are not on board with financial freedom.

The World Bank says no to Bitcoin
The World Bank said it would not help El Salvador's implementation of Bitcoin because of the "environmental and transparency deficiencies" of the leading cryptocurrency.

A World Bank spokesperson confirmed that the organization remains committed to supporting El Salvador in many ways for transparency and regulation of currencies. But that offer does not extend to assistance with Bitcoin implementation.

"Although the government approached us for help with bitcoin, this is not something the World Bank can support given its environmental and transparency shortcomings," the spokesperson said.

The response came about when El Salvador's finance minister, Alejandro Zelaya, contacted the World Bank to implement Bitcoin as a parallel currency to the dollar.

Neither Zelaya nor his colleagues have responded publicly to the World Bank's decision.

However, several prominent proponents of Bitcoin have expressed their views on the issue. Anthony Pompliano implied a cynical motivation by saying, "CORRECTION: The World Bank has not figured out how to make money from Bde ITCO. '

While Max Keizer, true to form, proceeded to use profanity to express his thoughts on the issue. Even accusing the World Bank of complicity in financial inequality.

The World Bank is a global financial organization made up of 189 member countries that provide loans and grants to impoverished countries for capital projects.

It has two goals, to end poverty in a sustainable way and to promote shared prosperity.

However, in 2006, a four-month investigation by the Government Project pointed out corruption at the World Bank.

The report estimated that more than 20% of the loans they made, about $4 billion, were tainted by corrupt practices.

Investigators also discovered several other problems at the organization, especially related to holding up internal investigations. For example, a structure that discourages reporting corrupt practices with punishment for whistleblowers.

Although this report is 15 years old, it still highlights the lack of accountability in high-level intergovernmental bodies.

Bitcoin coming to Uruguay?

There is more than a chance that El Salvador will have a successor in the form of Uruguay in terms of adopting bitcoin as legal tender. In fact, a Uruguayan senator has introduced a law that would convert cryptocurrencies into legal tender in the South American country.

The law presented on Tuesday by Senator Juan Sartori aims to provide legal, financial and fiscal security for the entire industry surrounding cryptocurrencies in Uruguay. "Crypto assets will be recognized and accepted by the law. Furthermore, they will be recognized as legal tender," the proposal states.

Cryptocurrencies are an opportunity for the economy After presenting the law, Juan Sartori let slip on Twitter, "Cryptocurrencies are an opportunity to attract investment and create jobs." So, like El Salvador, Uruguay sees the adoption of bitcoin as an opportunity to work itself into a better position economically. For countries whose weak economies and national currencies force them to choose either the U.S. dollar or bitcoin, it can certainly be interesting to at least try a combination.

The bill stipulates that any natural person or company may receive or send cryptocurrencies as legal tender. Both at their own bank and at licensed crypto service providers in Uruguay.

If the bill makes it to the finish line, the government will come up with an "initial license" that should allow companies to trade cryptocurrencies on exchanges. A second license should eventually allow companies to hold and store cryptocurrencies. A third license should allow companies to issue their own cryptocurrencies or tokens. What exactly we should expect from this is not yet entirely clear.

How likely is it that the bill will pass?
There are more often politicians with wild plans who use a bill to generate attention for their own campaign. Often these figures have a political minority and not the power to get a proposal through all the necessary gates. However, the same cannot be said about Juan Sartori and his National Party.

In fact, the coalition that Sartori and his National Party are in has a majority of 17 of the 30 seats in the Senate. So the Coalición Multicolor, as they go through life, does have the power to get the bill to the finish line. So there is certainly a chance that Uruguay will become the second country after El Salvador to have bitcoin recognized as legal tender.

Step by step, countries on the periphery of the financial system are beginning to recognize the potential economic lifeboat that bitcoin represents for them. Interestingly, countries do not have to go all-in at all to benefit from this. Without completely abandoning the conventional system in one fell swoop, they have the opportunity to quietly experiment with bitcoin to see what it does for the economy. As hodlers *(long term bitcoin holders)*, we obviously don't say no to this kind of development.

Bitcoin: worth more than one million?

Is it better to trade or hodl? That decision is entirely up to you. Therefore, in this analysis, there is something for everyone. We start with the short term, and then look at the long term perspective of bitcoin, based on the work of analyst Dave the Wave.

Average moves the wrong way
We'll start with the short term first, and that includes candles that represent a short period of time. In the chart below, each candle represents 4 hours. The green line is the moving average of the 50 candles, so of 200 hours. This is a relatively short period and that's why this is such an important indicator for the coming days. As you can see below, the bitcoin price has been dancing on this tightrope for two months. On several occasions in July, this proved to be a resistance that bitcoin just couldn't get above, until July 21.

The momentum changed and the price violently broke the short-term trend. The 50MA (moving average) changed from an unconquerable monster into a support zone. Meanwhile, the 50MA has turned into a resistance line again and for bitcoin to find its way up, the 50MA must be broken in the short term.

The long term of Dave the Wave
There are several models to say something about the long term of the bitcoin price. The two models of the Dutch analyst PlanB are incredibly popular. Dave the

27

Wave also offers an interesting model, and his work is often seen as the counterpart to what PlanB has created. Dave's thesis is that Bitcoin follows its logarithmic growth curve model. Logarithmic growth suggests exponential gains in the beginning that slowly decline in the long run.

He says that if bitcoin is worth more than $100 thousand in December this year, then the stock-to-flow model remains valid and its logarithmic growth curve is invalid. If bitcoin fails to reach that goal in December, then the reverse obviously applies. Dave goes on to say that bitcoin is an emerging currency, but that the road to success is not all uphill. He foresees periods of volatility in both directions, as new people add liquidity, but also take it out again. 'Bitcoin is following the path of gold that was capitalized for hundreds if not thousands of years, Bitcoin has already reached a market capitalization of $1 trillion in just 12 years.'

If the bitcoin price follows its logarithmic growth curve, bitcoin can expect a price of between 500 thousand and 1 million dollars in about ten years.

Explanation of his model

What are we looking at? This is a chart that covers almost the entire price history of bitcoin, each candle represents 1 month. The top part of the graph shows the price and the blue slanted lines shows the trend. Over each cycle Dave throws in the Fibonacci indicator, which are those thin, straight lines with those little numbers.

The Fibonacci sequence is a series of numbers that indicates a natural progression. It is common in nature and is also used in many mathematical models. Financial analysis does not escape it either. The series is very simple. Start at 0 and follow with 1, and further, now each subsequent number is the sum of the previous two. As an example: 0, 1, 1, 2, 3, 5, 8, 13, 21, and so on.

In the previous cycles, the bottom was at the Fibonacci level 0.618 and it must be reached before bitcoin can

29

think about a new all time high. This levelua is not arbitrary, but is the top of the previous cycle (20 thousand dollars). Bitcoin, according to this model, will descend to this level in the coming months.

Dave uses another indicator to reinforce this model, namely the LMACD. You can see this at the bottom of the chart and it is a modified version of the MACD, so it can also be used on Logarithmic scale (hence the L). The abbreviation stands for Moving Average Convergence Divergence. Where convergence and divergence are nice words for 'converging' and 'diverging'.

The blue line in this case is the LMACD and the orange line is called the signal line. So, the key here is to find the moments where the LMACD line and the signal line diverge (divergence), or converge (convergence). If the LMACD line dips below the signal line, Dave believes this signals that the peak of this cycle has been reached and it is a good time to sell. Conversely, of course, if the blue LMACD rises above the orange signal line, the bottom has been reached and bitcoin can expect a rise of many months.

The moments when the two lines intersect are indicated by a black circle.

What can you expect from bitcoin?
So Dave the Wave's model predicts that the peak of this cycle has already been and that bitcoin will descend to

20 thousand dollars in the coming months. It is bearish in the short term, but bullish in the long term.

Long term strategy for bitcoin?

So bitcoin has had another surge recently and now seems to be catching its breath with a price above $35,000. After months of consolidation, bitcoin seems ready for green price action again. High time to grab the blockchain data to see how the market has reacted to the first positive price movement in months.

The first thing to look at is the selling behavior of hodlers *(long term bitcoin holders)*. With the appearance of some green candlesticks, have they seen their chance to take profits or are they holding on tight to their bitcoin? In addition to analyzing the sentiment of hodlers *(long term bitcoin holders)*, we also dive deeper into the number of bitcoin on the major exchanges, which always makes for an interesting picture.

Are hodlers confident about the future?
After a long period of mediocre results for bitcoin, we finally shot up like a rocket this past week. The big question, of course, is how this rally has been received by seasoned bitcoiners. It seems that some of the hodlers have used this uptrend to take profits. Indeed, more than 1.5 billion dollars worth of profits have been liquidated on the blockchain.

Against that more than 1.5 billion dollars of realized profits, there were also more than 200 million dollars of realized losses. It is interesting to note that Glassnode's aSOPR statistic has been a good predictor of the stock price in recent times. This statistic measures the ratio of realized gains to losses in the bitcoin market that have been at the same address for more than one hour.

The aSOPR value of 1 has acted as a good resistance level in recent months. After last week's rally, we broke firmly through that barrier. Now, as far as the aSOPR is concerned, two scenarios are possible. The first scenario is that the value of 1 now becomes a support level, which would be bullish, and the other scenario is that we fall through the 1 and the bears take over again.

Number of bitcoin on exchanges continues to decline
This week was an unusual one when it comes to bitcoin outflows at exchanges. In fact, since November of last year, not as many bitcoin have disappeared from the major exchanges as in the past week. In fact, we were at a pace where about 100,000 bitcoin per month would

flow out of the exchanges toward the on-chain wallets of hodlers.

In total, the major exchanges now have only 13.2 percent of all bitcoin in circulation in their wallets. To which you must also add that many retail investors hodge their bitcoin with an exchange. Over the past few months, bitcoin at the major exchange platforms went up, but that trend has now firmly reversed again.

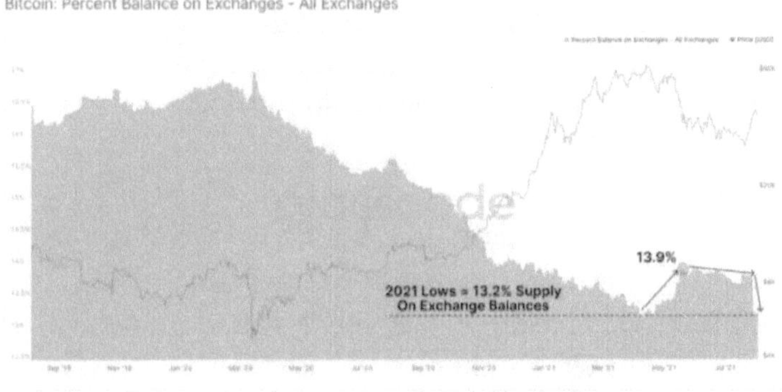

Another interesting fact is the dynamic between Coinbase and Binance. For the vast majority of 2021, Coinbase was the exchange with the most outflows of the two, and Binance even experienced frequent inflows. Now, at least for Binance, that seems to have reversed, as the exchange saw an outflow of about 37,500 bitcoin this week. Coinbase had to make do with an outflow of 31,000 bitcoin. Is another supply squeeze coming? That wouldn't be a bad thing!

How to get rich with bitcoin?

In 10 years, almost all bitcoins will be mined, meaning you might only need 0.022 BTC to be considered stinking rich. This is what a writer from Omgfin Exchange argues.

Investment of 900 dollars is enough
At the current bitcoin rate, a purchase of 0.022 bitcoin costs about 900 dollars depending on the current price ofcourse, but the writer says current trends in global wealth distribution and the inevitable limited supply of bitcoin could mean that this could be worth up to a million in the future.

Opinions are divided on that, by the way, and is not actually relevant to the rest of this article. By the way, the article was based on last year's situation, we will use the latest known numbers.

Millionaires own 46% of all wealth
According to Credit Suisse's Global Wealth Report 2021, there are 56.1 million individuals with a net worth of more than $1 million. The index takes into account a person's wealth, as well as all the assets they have invested in, while subtracting debts and liabilities.

Despite representing only 1% of the world's population (not counting children), millionaires own 46% of the world's wealth.

According to Credit Suisse's individual wealth distribution, 215,300 people were worth more than 50 million. And of these, another 68,010 people were worth at least 100 million, and 5,332 even had assets of more than $500 million.

Fair distribution of bitcoin

Currently, there are 18,775,881 bitcoins mined, which means there are 2,224,118 more to come. In 10 years, the supply will be 20.6 million, or 98% of the 21 million coins in the total supply. Also, take into account the 1.6 million coins (8.78% according to Glassnode's HodlWaves) that have not been touched for more than a decade, which in practice leaves a limit of 19 million bitcoin for all the world's millionaires.

Then you end up with 0.34 bitcoin per millionaire, including the coins that have yet to be mined. For this thought experiment, we assume a proportional distribution among only the millionaires.

But we can tighten this up even further. If we subtract from this all the bitcoins that have not been moved for five years or more, you are left with only 16 million BTC. In this scenario, each of the world's millionaires could own only 0.37 bitcoin each.

In addition to the true millionaires, there are 583 million individuals with assets between $100 thousand and $1 million. These people should not be ignored as potential holders, even if their purchasing power is lower.

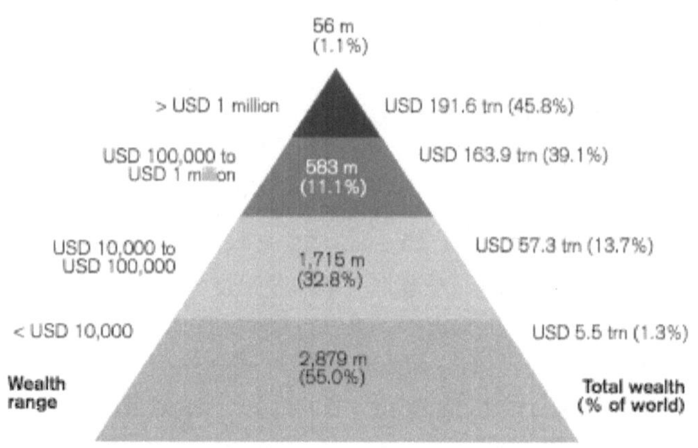

Based on wealth distribution

Assuming the global wealth share in the above graph remains the same, millionaires represent 7.3 million coins (45.8%) out of the total stock of bitcoin (minus lost coins). There are 56.1 million millionaires according to the report so this works out to 0.13 bitcoin per millionaire.

The remaining 583 million individuals who are currently worth 100 thousand to a million could effectively own another 6.3 million coins.

37

That makes a total of 13.6 million bitcoins, divided by the tonnners + millionaires, you end up with 0.022 bitcoin per high net individual.

What can you tentatively conclude with this thought experiment? That with a 900 dollar investment in bitcoin at the current rate, you can be at the top of the fiat pyramid.

The best cryptocurrencies of 2021

1. Bitcoin

Without a doubt, Bitcoin has become the most popular and well-known crypto currency in the world.

Many merchants and businesses already accept Bitcoin as payment. For example, Bitcoin is already accepted as a valid means of payment at Microsoft and the Burger Kind.

Bitcoin aims to remove control from central organizations such as central banks and governments in payment systems. Thus, every transaction is visible to everyone.

Bitcoin is one big project that different teams and developers continue to work on. A developer can do his or her part by participating in startup projects.

In this book we discussed the recent news surrounding bitcoin and what to expect for 2021, all and all it makes a very solid investment for the long and short term.

Short term for making profit with active trading and long term to make sure a part of your savings will be safe from inflation.

2. Ethereum

Ethereum (ETH) is considered the most popular crypto currency after Bitcoin.

Ethereum has some similarities to Bitcoin, but it can do even more.

Namely, Ethereum's transfers are faster than Bitcoin's and Ethereum's blockchain technology can handle more transactions.

In addition, unlike Bitcoin, Ethereum also supports "smart contract" technology. This is a secure way of entering into digital agreements without first building a mutual trust. Bitcoin is only focused on digital transactions.

Last and most important, Ethereum can also create centralized apps (dApps). Using blockchain technology, these dApps run on a decentralized platform with no central authority.

For example, services like Facebook and Whatsapp are centralized. So your messages are under the control of these authorities. With dApps, this is not the case.

Ethereum is also seen as a new era of the internet; an internet that is not controlled by one company or person and where users can own their own data.

Ethereum price expectation
Estimating the price expectation of Ethereum is difficult. At the beginning of the new year, the price skyrocketed, but like Bitcoin, it has also partially plummeted again.

Ethereum is currently in full development. The number of developers and collaborations are growing rapidly. Eventually this could mean that more people will use Ethereum, which could result in a price increase. Whether this will actually happen we do not know for sure.

A good influence on the price will be the upgrade discussed in the chapter later on in the book. we advice you to read to make sure you can make a proper assessment on an investment in Ethereum.

3. Cardano

Cardano is known as the third generation blockchain and was founded by the co-founder of Ethereum. Cardano is therefore very similar to Ethereum.

The purpose of Cardano is to carry out financial applications that can be used by millions of consumers worldwide, for example by companies, consumers and governments.

Cardano is so far the only currency where the blockchain has been developed where scientific research has been done to see where the problems lie in practice.

The blockchain was built by a team of engineers and academics (experts in the industry).

Cardano is still in the process of development. So it will not happen soon that you can pay with Cardano within a year.

Difference Proof of Stake (Pos) and Proof of Work (Pow) Two techniques are used to validate transactions:

- Proof of work
- Proof of stake

How does Proof of work work?
The person who does the most work to solve a problem gets a reward. This is called mining. To validate transactions, miners must solve a mathematical puzzle. With each new block, the puzzle becomes more difficult and thus more energy is consumed.

Examples: Bitcoin and Litecoin

How does Proof of stake work?
The person with the largest number of coins in the network validates the transactions and receives a reward. This also takes into account how long investors have held the coins. There is no mining in this mechanism, as all coins have already been created.

Example: Cardano

Cardano, unlike Bitcoin for example, works with Proof of Stake (PoS). The major advantage of this is that much less computing power is required and therefore less power is consumed per transaction. As a result, transaction costs decrease.

The advantages for Cardano
Adaptable - Adjustments can be made easily. This allows the technology behind Cardano to be improved relatively quickly.

Regulatory cooperation - Cardano tries to take into account the regulations in different countries.

Tight future plan - In 2021, there are many projects planned for this company; improving smart contracts, adding scalability and improving decision making.

Disadvantages of Cardano
The project is still under development - There are not very many features available at this time. The project has yet to prove itself.

Cardano future expectation
It is also difficult for Cardano to estimate where it is going in the future.

Most experts are positive about the future. Indeed, the Cardano team continues to improve its blockchain at a rapid pace.

4. Binance Coin
The Binance Coin works differently from all the other crypto currencies mentioned in this article.

The Binance Coin is the coin of the popular crypto platform Binance. On Binance, you can sell and buy all known crypto currencies. By using the Binance Coin on the platform when buying and selling cryptocurrencies, you get a discount. The Binance Coin was launched in July 2017 and is similar to Bitcoin.

Benefits of the Binance Coin
Low transaction fees - Using the Binance coin keeps the cost of your transactions low.

Destruction of coins - Binance burns coins every so often. This means that the supply gets smaller. Should the demand grow then the price of the coin grows.

Depending on popularity Binance - The value of Binance coin depends on the platform Binance. It is expected that Binance will continue to grow in the coming years and so will the value of the coin.

Disadvantages of the Binance Coin
Discount will disappear in the future - Binance has announced that the discount on transaction fees will disappear after 5 years.

Binance Coin price forecast
An exact prediction on the price ter expectation for Binance Coin cannot be made.

Experts believe that the Binance Coin price will increase significantly in the coming years because of the growing popularity of the exchange platform.

Do you want to buy Binance Coin? When buying, always keep an eye on all Binance Coin news for any developments.

5. Polkadot

Polkadot was founded by Gavin Wood, co-founder of Ethereum. It was a reaction to the slow development of Ethereum and he therefore started the Web3 Foundation.

Polkadot is a shared multichain network that connects multiple blockchains into a unified network.

This allows these independent blockchains to share information and transactions. Users can thus combine information from different blockchains.

The goal of Polkadot is to realize a fully decentralized web where users have full control and ownership of their data and identity instead of the Internet monopolies.

The advantages of Polkadot
Unique mechanism - Polkadot distinguishes itself through a shared mechanism where several independent blockchains can work together. Thus,

applications from Ethereum, Bitcoin and Cardano, for example, can also be used within Polkadot.

Sharding - Processing and verifying transactions do not have to be approved by the entire network but can be distributed across the network. This makes transactions fast and cheap.

Customizable - Each blockchain can be customized and is easy to update. Development teams can thus optimize their network in terms of finance, gaming, IoT, social networks etc. Already 350 projects are actively building on the network.

The disadvantages of Polkadot
Young project - Polkadot was launched in May 2020. So the project is not even 1 year old yet.

The future of Polkadot
In just a few months, Polkadot has risen relatively quickly, only to fall sharply all at once.

Still, experts believe that the rise will continue in the coming years, but making an exact long-term prediction is difficult in the cryptocurrency market.

6. Chainlink

Chainlink was founded in 2017 by fintech company SmartContract. Chainlink wants to make smart contracts available to the whole world.

Chainlink has solved a problem that Ethereum runs into. The problem is that external data cannot be incorporated into a smart contract.

Chainlink provides a link between smart contracts (agreements) and blockchain platforms. Through an oracle, external data can still be processed in a contract.

An oracle sends external data (what happens in the real world) to the blockchain, so that this data can be used.

Chainlink already works with SWIFT, Gartner and Google.

The advantages of Chainlink
Unique position - There is no other crypto currency that offers the same application as Chainlink.

Suitable for all platforms - It works with both Bitcoin, Ethereum etc. So it doesn't matter which coin becomes the most successful.

Connection to the real world - Chainlink allows you to connect the real world and smart contracts.

The disadvantages of Chainlink
Less reliable - By using external data, reliability is compromised. This is because the owner of the source of the external data can modify the data to influence the contract.

Success dependent on large companies - For the project
to succeed, large companies must partner with
Chainlink.

No future plan - The company has not published a
roadmap, so it is unclear what they plan to do in the
coming year or years.

The future of Chainlink
Like other cryptocurrencies, the price of Chainlink has
also risen and fallen significantly in recent months.

The price expectations of Chainlink from experts are
positive. An expert in crypto currencies says that
Chainlink could be worth as much as 100 dollars by the
end of 2025.

7. Litecoin

Litecoin has been around since 2012 and has been a
staple of the top 10 cryptocurrencies since then.
Litecoin was founded by a former Google employee
Charlie Lee and is very similar to Bitcoin.

Litecoin's goal is to make payments faster and cheaper
than Bitcoin. Like Bitcoin, it uses blockchain technology
which puts banks and governments out of business
when it comes to payments.

Litecoin, like Bitcoin, is also accepted by some
companies as a means of payment.

The benefits of Litecoin
Decentralization - Transactions are stored on the blockchain just like Bitcoin. Thus, there is no central authority controlling Litecoin.

Fast transactions - A transaction with Litecoin takes place after 2.5 minutes vs. 10 minutes with Bitcoin.

Cheap transactions - In addition, the average transaction fee is $0.01. In comparison, Bitcoin has average transaction fees of $3.

Adaptable - Changes to the protocol can be made quickly.

The disadvantages of Litecoin
Used on the Dark Web - Litecoin is one of the most widely used crypto currency on the Dark Web. This fact is not a good marketing for the coin.

Litecoin owner sold all his Litecoins - Charlie Lee sold all his coins in December 2017 when the price was high. As a result, the crypto currency lost credibility for a time.

The financial future of Litecoin
The expectations of the price of Litecoin vary widely, but almost all are positive. As you can see, the Litecoin price has risen significantly in recent months, and has fallen significantly again.

The Litecoin price is highly dependent on the Bitcoin price. Is the Bitcoin rising? Then there is a good chance that the Litecoin price will also rise.

8. XRP

Ripple (XRP) focuses on enabling fast and cheap payments through a decentralized platform.

It is a peer-to-peer network for international money transfers and provides financial institutions with a digital payment protocol.

Instead of putting banks out of business, it actually enters into collaborations with various banks and financial institutions. A large number of organizations have already supported Ripple, including Santander Bank and American Express.

Unlike other cryptos, Ripple does not work with blockchain technology. Ripple has developed its own technology to process and verify transactions: Ripple Protocol Consensus Algorithm (RPCA).

This has the feature of making transactions relatively cheap and consuming less power.

The advantages of Ripple

Instant transactions - Ripple can process payments within 5 seconds by using a network of servers.

Versatility - Ripple is not trying to replace a payment system, but to work with financial institutions. Thus, it can be used to exchange any currency, including crypto.

Extremely low transaction fees - The transaction fee of a payment is $0.0001. Compared to other crypto currencies, this is extremely cheap.

Aimed at financial institutions and banks - The technology is intended to introduce a new digital payment protocol, addressing the problems of current payment systems.

The disadvantages of Ripple
Large token holders have a lot of power - The company owns as much as 70% of the coins giving them a position of power. Thus, they can single-handedly cause the price to drop or rise.

Ongoing lawsuit against Ripple - The outcome of this lawsuit can have a major effect on the price of Ripple. If there is a negative outcome, it could even mean the end of Ripple.

The financial future of Ripple
Unfortunately, it is impossible to make a price forecast of the future for Ripple or other crypto currencies in this volatile market.

The expectations of experts vary widely. Half foresee no problems and the other half see the price falling away (even to 0). The outcome of the court case will have an impact on the price. This result is expected before August 16, 2021.

Bitcoin versus Ethereum

What is the difference and which cryptocurrency has the most promising future?

Earlier we explained how Bitcoin has tremendous long-term potential but how does it hold up against the number 2. Should you invest in both coins?

Bitcoin and Ethereum are the two largest crypto-currencies in market capitalization. Co-investors often choose to hold only one of the two in their portfolio. Despite that approach, these crypto currencies are still very different. What are the biggest differences? Why do people believe in one, and not the other? A few industry experts shed their light on the matter.

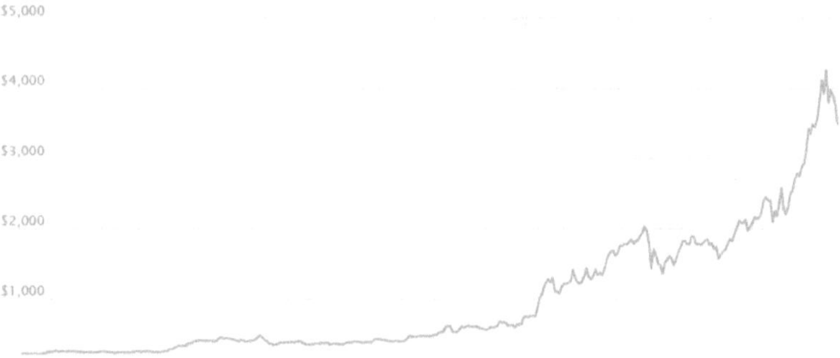

The bull-run of Ethereum in the past year

2021 has so far proved to be the year of Ethereum. The second crypto currency is rapidly approaching Bitcoin's market capitalization. For example, with a market capitalization of $501 billion, the currency is more valuable than U.S. investment bank JP Morgan at the time of writing.

Still, Bitcoin's biggest challenger has a long way to go if it wants to outgrow the market capitalization of Bitcoin (currently at $1 trillion). Recently, 1 Bitcoin was worth a whopping 13.25 Ethereum.

What exactly is Ethereum?

The Ethereum coin (ETH) is one of the coins with the most market capitalization. A high market capacity usually indicates that there is a lot of faith in a particular coin, and the Ethereum coin, like Bitcoin, has a lot of faith.

Whereas investors are skeptical about the future of Bitcoin, the future of the Ethereum coin appears to be bright for the time being. Indeed, the price of the Ethereum currency increased by more than 3000 percent in 2017.

Of course, the question is always whether investing in this virtual currency is still worthwhile. To be able to answer this question for yourself, this page will explain the principle of the currency. This way you can get an idea of what kind of currency it is and how you see the future of Ethereum.

How does it differ from Bitcoin?

Where Ripple, for example, focuses on making transactions faster for the financial market, the Ethereum coin focuses on the use of applications. The principle of Ethereum technology is to create a situation in which applications can be used without the intervention of a central authority. The applications that use this technology are also called DApps (or Decentralized Apps). The main advantage of applications using Ethereum technology is that there is basically no more data loss, manipulation of data, censorship within the application or downtime of the application.

The Ethereum currency's price is determined by more than just supply and demand among investors. The price is much more dependent on how much use is made of the DApps. A large number of businesses around the world support the Ethereum concept. As a result, it is not surprising that the currency's value has risen dramatically in 2017.

In the cryptocurrency market, Ethereum is still a relatively new coin. Ethereum's price has steadily increased since its inception in 2015. In 2017, the price of Ethereum increased by more than 3000 percent. This rise was easily explained as more international companies expressed interest in Ethereum.

Multinational corporations such as ING, Microsoft, BP, and Deloitte, to name a few, have already joined the Enterprise Ethereum Alliance (a partnership founded by Ethereum). The world's largest corporations are increasingly interested in collaborating with Ethereum. When more large companies that use the Ethereum network, the more trust there is in the currency. Higher confidence, of course, results in a higher exchange rate.

Purchasing Ethereum coins is similar to purchasing Bitcoin. Ethereum is linked to all of the well-known "Cryptocurrency exchanges," making it extremely simple to purchase the coin with other cryptocurrencies.

Purchasing Ethereum is similar to purchasing Bitcoin. Ethereum is linked to all of the well-known "Cryptocurrency exchanges," making it extremely simple to purchase the coin with other cryptocurrencies.

Ethereum coins can also be purchased with dollars through a number of international providers. Because not all exchanges charge a reasonable transaction fee, it is best to stick with the more well-known parties. The trick to buying Ethereum coins is, of course, to wait for the right time to buy. Many investors buy the coins when they are on the verge of falling in value.

The Ethereum cryptocurrency is relatively stable (as far as a Crypto currency can be stable). Despite the fact that the coin is relatively stable, investing in cryptocurrency is always risky.

As a result, only invest in Ethereum with funds that you can afford to lose. Many people believe that it is necessary to purchase full Ethereum coins; however, this is not the case. You can also purchase a half-coin or less.

Ethereum coins can be deposited using either an online or offline wallet. For the online deposit of Ethereum coins, you have a large number of online wallet providers to choose from.

Ethereum can be purchased online through exchanges such as Binance. Because Ethereum coins have a relatively high value, more people are opting to keep their coins safe and secure offline. You can also choose between a hardware wallet and a mobile wallet.

NFT and Ethereum

One of the reasons that Ethereum might see a good price increase in the next few years is because of NFT (non-fungible tokens).

NFTs have become wildly popular in a short time, including among artists hoping to earn a little pocket change in coronation times. Or pocket change? Some NFT art changes hands for millions.

The hype around non-fungible tokens is attracting newcomers to the crypto world. They are curious about what NFTs are or hope to become rich quickly by trading in digital art.

NFT sales run primarily over the Ethereum platform, like Bitcoin a decentralized network based on the blockchain concept. But just having a digital wallet full of ether - one of the most popular crypto currencies - doesn't get you there.

If you want to read more about NFT art and trading NFTs you can check out our book on the subject.

Summary:

- Ethereum is a decentralized platform that uses the blockchain technology pioneered by the mysterious Satoshi Nakamoto - a pseudonym - creator of Bitcoin.
- 'Whereas Bitcoin has discovered a way to transfer value digitally, directly from person to person, Ethereum is taking a different approach,' writes the niche website BTC.direct. The Ethereum network is said to be the foundation of a new type of Internet. Importantly, the Ethereum 'ecosystem' serves as a foundation for the development of decentralized applications (DAPPs) and smart contracts.
- DAPPs would be much more privacy-friendly and secure than current centralized Internet applications. They are also uncensorable.

How do big Ethereum investors see the future?

Tally Greenberg, head of business development at software company Allnodes has the following to say about Ethereum:

'The technological advantage and utility of the Ethereum ecosystem is far greater than that of Bitcoin, and I think investors are beginning to see that too. There is currently more than $75 billion invested in DeFi projects on the Ethereum blockchain - just a month ago

it was $40 billion. Just the smart contracts supported by the network offer endless possibilities and should be enough for Ethereum to have a competitive advantage over Bitcoin.'

Steve Ehrlich, CEO and founder of cryptocurrency brokerage Voyager Digital:

"I believe Ethereum offers better prospects due to its utility, functionality, and ecosystem." Clients of Voyager (crypto asset broker, ed.) who own both Bitcoin and Ether have begun to hold more Ether in recent months. We are also seeing that our larger investors are becoming more comfortable with Ether's risk/reward profile. The Ethereum blockchain is powering the most developed ecosystem for decentralized finance and NFTs, which are all gaining popularity. Ethereum will also receive a -interesting- upgrade in the near future."

"There is anticipation that ETH will be recognized by institutional investors," **says Megan Kaspar, managing director of crypto investment firm Magnetic.**

"Ether, I believe, will gain traction. When investors become aware of the technological opportunities, capital flows will shift to Ether. In the long run, technical and fundamental analyses show that Ether has a higher upside potential than Bitcoin."

What is the difference between Bitcoin and Ethereum?

The Ethereum network allows developers to build their own decentralized applications; Bitcoin does not have this.

Another difference is that the creator of Ethereum is known, while that of Bitcoin is not.

Supply determines the price of Bitcoin (unlike fiat currency, the supply Bitcoins is scarce and finite). With Ether, however, there are other factors at play: for example, the network allows start-ups to issue a token for their own blockchain project.

Right now, investors should have both Bitcoin and Ethereum in their portfolios.

Bitcoin has a strong chance of remaining the world's leading crypto asset, while Ethereum has a sTrong chance of becoming the world's leading distributed software development platform.

As a result, if you want to get the most out of your portfolio, **invest in both now.**

The upgrade for Ethereum in 2021

August 5 is the date: the long-awaited upgrade of the Ethereum network will go ahead. Initially it was supposed to happen on August 4, but the project was delayed by a day.

The upgrade is named "London hardfork" and will be performed on block number 12,965,000 of the Ethereum blockchain.

Some long-awaited improvements, called Ethereum Improvement Proposals, will be implemented. The best known of these is the controversial EIP-1559.

There are four things you need to know about the upcoming upgrade to the Ethereum network.

1. EIP-1559 should make transaction costs more predictable
Transaction costs on the Ethereum network have risen astronomically since the beginning of this year, in part due to the increasing popularity of decentralized finance, or DeFi. This replaces a range of centralized and regulated financial institutions with decentralized systems and products generally built on the Ethereum blockchain.

Ethereum developers want to solve the increasing transaction costs with a series of changes.

In the current system, users have to pay a fee in order for a transaction to go through. They get to decide how high that fee in (although there is a minimum amount). The more you pay, the faster the transaction takes place. Users bid against each other.

This can lead to hefty costs, because the value of ether in euros or dollars can fluctuate considerably. There is some time between the placement of a transaction and its processing. If the value of ether has risen considerably during that period, this can lead to unforeseen costs.

August 5 is the date: the long-awaited upgrade of the Ethereum network goes ahead. Initially it was supposed to happen on August 4, but the project was delayed by a day.

The upgrade is named "London hardfork" and will be performed on block number 12,965,000 of the Ethereum blockchain.

Some long-awaited improvements, called Ethereum Improvement Proposals, will be implemented. The best known of these is the controversial EIP-1559.

1. EIP-1559 should make transaction costs more predictable
Transaction costs on the Ethereum network have risen astronomically since the beginning of this year, in part due to the increasing popularity of decentralized

finance, or DeFi. This replaces a range of centralized and regulated financial institutions with decentralized systems and products generally built on the Ethereum blockchain.

Ethereum developers want to solve the increasing transaction costs with a series of changes.

In the current system, users have to pay a fee in order for a transaction to go through. They get to decide how high that fee in (although there is a minimum amount). The more you pay, the faster the transaction takes place. Users bid against each other.

This can lead to hefty costs, because the value of ether in euros or dollars can fluctuate considerably. There is some time between the placement of a transaction and its processing. If the value of ether has risen considerably during that period, this can lead to unforeseen costs.

Ethereum developers are also working on so-called sharding: splitting the blockchain into multiple chains. This should greatly increase the transaction speed and capacity of the network.

Why does Ripple get attention?

Aside from Bitcoin, there are a plethora of other cryptocurrencies that may be far more lucrative in terms of returns than the well-known Bitcoin. Ripple (XRP), is one of the cryptocurrencies with a massive market cap. Since the end of 2017, the price of the Ripple currency has risen dramatically, and it continues to fluctuate significantly to this day.

You may be wondering, "Is the Ripple a good coin to invest in?" In order to provide a satisfactory answer, we will delve deeper into everything Ripple in this chapter.

What is Ripple?

Let us begin by answering the question, "What is Ripple?" Cryptocurrencies were developed in the aftermath of the economic crisis, partly to reduce the influence of banks on economic transactions. Whereas most cryptocurrencies today still base their profiles on this concept, the Ripple coin does not. Ripple, on the other hand, is a centralized currency designed to allow financial institutions (including banks) and international transactions to be completed more quickly.

Ripple is already working on a payment system solution for much of Santander's, Reise Bank's, BBVA's, Bank of America's, and UniCredit's banking traffic, among others. They already have a 40% stake in the payment system for banks in Asia.

Ripple's technology is expected to pique the interest of an increasing number of banks. As a result, the number of banks that will use this technology is expected to grow rapidly.

Of course, "speeding up international transactions" does not sound very clear right now. The principle of the Ripple technology will be explained in greater detail using a brief example: There is a currency difference when a customer wants to make a transaction from a Spanish bank (e.g., Santander) to an American bank (e.g. Bank of America).

The Spanish customer transfers the amount in euros, and this arrives in dollars at the American bank. In order to carry out these transactions, Santander Bank has an account with Bank of America and Bank of America has an account with Santander bank, so-called nostro and vostro accounts.

Making a Spanish payment to a U.S. bank takes a long time due to the many links in this process. Ripple focuses on speeding up this process, by completing transactions in Ripple currency.

Making a payment now no longer takes several days, but only a few seconds. Not only does this reduce transaction costs for banks, but customers of the banks can also complete their transactions faster.

The Ripple lawsuit

The SEC filed a surprise lawsuit against Ripple and two of its executives, co-founder Chris Larsen and CEO Brad Garlinghouse, in December. The regulator claims that continuing to sell XRP to individual investors violates securities laws.

The SEC hopes to strengthen its case by demonstrating that Ripple purposefully manipulated the cryptocurrency's XRP price expectation with strategically timed announcements.

So far, Larsen and Garlinghouse's analysis of crypto wallets has revealed that massive amounts of XRP were delivered to exchanges based on foreign soil. However, Ripple "did not hand over any non-U.S. based digital asset account documents or otherwise explain the significance of these XRP transfers," according to the SEC letter.

"Although the SEC has also attempted to obtain this information directly from Ripple, Ripple recently informed the SEC that Ripple does not have it either, leaving the only avenue for investigation offshore," the letter explains.

However, it appears that the investigations are not off to a good start, with requests to nine different foreign regulators returning empty-handed. According to the letter, two regulators refused to help, and three others refused to allow the SEC to publish their communications. Only one regulator suggested that the

SEC could use conversations between the two parties to strengthen its case.

If the court grants Ripple's motion, the SEC would be required to make cease and desist requests to foreign regulators, effectively ending this line of inquiry.

11:20
Bitcoin
$36,588.28
-0.02%
$38,769.84

What is the price of Ripple?

Now that we've covered the fundamentals and the recent news surrounding the lawsuit against Ripple, let's get to the bottom of the question: What is the price of Ripple? Ripple was founded in 2012 with the goal of speeding up financial transactions. Whereas the price was initially stable (low), it has risen significantly since the end of 2017.

Ripple became a billion-dollar company almost immediately as a result of the price increase. The owners of Ripple still manage a large portion of the market capacity, so the public has only a limited amount of market capacity.

The price rise can be explained by the fact that Ripple has contracted with a number of large customers in the financial world. These include customers such as Bank of America and Royal Bank of Scotland. In addition, Ripple has the support of many multinational companies, including Google. In January 2018, the price first stood at $3.10 per Ripple.

The price increase can be explained by the fact that Ripple has signed contracts with a number of large financial customers. Customers include Bank of America and the Royal Bank of Scotland. Furthermore, Ripple has the backing of many multinational corporations, including Google. In January 2018, the price was $3.10 per Ripple.

How to buy Ripple

Are you already a little excited? Then you must be asking yourself, where can I buy Ripple? In the beginning, it was difficult to buy Ripple with dollars or euros. Fortunately, more and more options for this have emerged recently.

When buying Ripple coins with dollars, there are often high transaction fees. It is therefore advisable to first convert the dollars to a more common digital currency (for example, Bitcoin (BTC) or Ethereum (ETH) and then purchase the Ripple coins through an exchange like Binance.

How to develop your trading strategy

How should you develop your own Crypto trading strategy? Of course with the help of Stellar Moon Publishing! A good crypto trading strategy gives you handholding, focus, peace of mind and not least: a delicious amount of profit. Since we suspect that this is of interest to many, today we'll take a deeper look at elements that determine an ultimate trading strategy.

There is no single trading strategy that works for everyone. A trading strategy will only be successful when it is optimally attuned to you as a person, what kind of trader you are, your capital, your risk profile, et cetera. That's why we specifically look at the underlying elements.

In this way you will come to a crypto trading strategy which closely matches you as a person, with all the opportunities and risks that fit to who you are and what kind of trader you want to be. Got curious? Let's go!

Attention: keep in mind that the following explanation about developing a Crypto trading strategy and the explanation of this should in no way be interpreted as advice.

The choice for if and in which way you want to trade crypto and which choices you're going to make regarding buying and selling lies with you and you alone.

What exactly is a crypto trading strategy?
A crypto trading strategy is a previously drawn up personal plan to which you commit yourself while trading. In short, they are guidelines or rules, which you keep yourself to while trading.

By doing so you'll prevent crazy jumps, impulsive purchases and sales, significant losses which you can't cover, emotions which take over from you and a feeling that you're "all over the place" with your trading methods.

A trading strategy is not only a guideline when you want to take a position (buy) or close a position (sell), but it also focuses on much less tangible elements such as a personal risk profile or personal preference regarding timeframes.

Still, it is not mere feeling and preference that rules the roost. On the contrary. Many elements of a successful trading strategy have been founded on rock-solid data, figures, analyses, charts and prediction models (and trading indicators). So, do you like statistical analysis? Then you can have a lot of fun putting down and opting for a successful trading strategy.

What makes a Trading strategy successful?
The ultimate trading strategy has a few extremely important characteristics. We list a few of them for you.

A successful trading strategy:

- is up to date
- is personal
- is in line with a (correct) Technical Analysis (TA)
- fits your risk profile

We're sure there are more characteristics to invent, but it may be clear that a good trading strategy today, may literally be worthless tomorrow. It may also be clear that the trading strategy which works fantastic for the first person, but this trading strategy won't work out for someone else, because you is a completely different kind of trader.

That's why it's also risky to invest (a lot of) money for a trading strategy of someone else, because this strategy doesn't take into account your own situation and preferences. You can find countless videos of (supposedly) successful daytraders, forex traders and crypto traders, who are sharing their ultimate trading strategy with you on YouTube.

Sometimes for a lot of money, sometimes for free. Sometimes as an expert, sometimes as a hobby. Free advice is not necessarily worse than expensive advice.

But do you want the best trading strategy which suits you so well and takes into account everything you want to put into crypto trading and achieve? Then you'll have to put in the time and energy yourself. And quite honestly: achieving success on something you've built and invented yourself is the best feeling in the world. But what then are important elements in a successful trading strategy?

Key elements of a successful trading strategy

Our crypto experts generally apply these 6 key elements which in our opinion, fit within a successful trading strategy. They provide a solid foundation, they are flexible and they guarantee a dynamic character so that the trading strategy is and remains sustainable. We'll list them down below and then briefly explain them.

1. **Trading rules**
2. **Risk Management**
3. **Trading Timeframes**
4. **Technical Analysis (TA)**
5. **Back testing**
6. **Reinventing yourself**

#1: Trading rules

Trading rules are rules that you impose on yourself. A successful crypto trading strategy stands or falls with the discipline you subsequently exercise whether or not you keep yourself to those rules. If you notice that you're not keeping to your own rules, you'll run an increased risk of getting surprises and risks which could turn out to be bad. With trading rules you can think of the following rules for instance:

I'm never allowed to have more than X% of my capital in open positions.

I lower that percentage by X% after 3 losing trades in a row.
I may only enter into a trade if it has been noted in my logbook.
I use a stop-loss of maximum X% of my purchase price.

Depending on your risk profile (calm down, just ten more seconds of patience), you can fill in a number at the place of the X which corresponds with the kind of trader you are.

The greater the risk you dare to take, the greater your profits or losses may turn out to be. However, it is wise not to let them exceed 3% in the case of the first 2 points.

#2: Risk Management
Risk management (or your risk profile) is, of all these elements, most in line with the personal level of your trading strategy.

One person is enormously risk-averse, the other person on the contrary loves the thrill and likes to explore the limits. As a rule of thumb applies: the more risk you take, the bigger the profits or the bigger the losses could be. Conversely, the less risk you take, the smaller the profits or losses can be.

Do you invest only with a certain percentage of your savings? Or with all your savings? Or with all the money you own at all? Or do you even take out an extra

79

mortgage on your house and then start trading with every cent you own that represents value?

As you'll understand, the risk you're taking in each of the above mentioned situations varies a lot.

With every trade you should ask yourself the question: What will happen if I completely lose this deposit? Can I miss this money? What would I do in that case?

#3: Trading Timeframes
It goes without saying that a strategy also has to fit in with the kind of trader you are. We briefly distinguish three different types of traders:

Day trader *(several trades per day)*
Swing trader *(trades which are open for days, weeks or months)*
Investor *(long term trader / HODL'er)*

Whereas a day trader is constantly looking at the numbers to spot every subtle change in price and opportunity or threat, an investor will mainly spend a lot of time looking for that ultimate long-term opportunity that looks promising and then leave his investment alone for a longer period. A Swing trader is a bit in between here.

A day trader doesn't take more or less risk than an investor, it's just a form that is much more intensive, but because of that can also yield more. Some traders also choose a dual trading strategy, which is aimed at an investor component (for example HODL on Bitcoin) and a day or swing trader component in which there is active trading (on Altcoins for example).

So it is important to determine for yourself what type of trader you are and what timeframes are important for you to follow.

For a day trader for instance these timeframes are the 4 hours, the 1 hour and the 15 minutes, whereas for a swing trader these timeframes are the 1 month, 1 week and 1 day. But also, different day traders can use different timeframes. Even here it is again very personal.

#4: Technical Analysis (TA)
Element number four has a strong connection with the first one, the trading rules. In this element you'll mainly determine on the basis of which indicators, candlesticks, patterns, et cetera you're going to take or sell your positions.

Questions which you'll ask yourself fall into the categories:

- **Which indicators must give a green light before I may take a position?**
- **Which indicators should give a negative signal before I'm going to sell a position?**

- **Which candlesticks are decisive for me in determining momentum?**
- **Which crypto will I invest in, or will I deliberately ignore?**

Technical analysis is also strongly linked to the fifth element. Or maybe the fifth element is just part of technical analysis.

#5: Back testing

Back testing is a technique or activity in which you can test how those variables would have performed in the past based on variables you set yourself. Even though past results are no guarantee for the future, it does add value to determine whether you are thinking in the right direction with certain trading rules.

Backtesting is therefore an excellent way of designing, optimizing or throwing away a conceived crypto trading strategy.

#6: Reinventing yourself

Once you have found your ultimate trading strategy with elements 1 through 5, it's time to reap the maximum benefits from it. So employ this strategy (within your risk profile) as thick as possible in order to maximize your profits. As it happens before you know it, your strategy has been outdated and you should start all over again.

That's why there is also element number 6. A strategy that didn't work in the past may suddenly turn out to be a gold mine in the future. A strategy that works brilliantly for your neighbor doesn't have to work for you. Always remain critical of market developments and their effect on your strategy. And dare to sharpen your strategy in between, where possible.

The best metaphor we can use for this is the metaphor of the lumberjack. You can cut many more trees as a lumberjack if you don't just keep chopping trees all day, but if you take a break every now relax so you can stay sharp.

How to choose the right trading strategy?
In case you were hoping for an 'easy trick' with which you could become shamelessly rich, then unfortunately we have bad news for you. There is no easy trick or everyone would do it. Of course, you could always unexpectedly stumble upon a huge windfall or a fortunate market development, but that would be more luck than wisdom.

A proper crypto trading strategy is tailor-made, and it is closely connected to your personal situation. That's why you can't always use the 'perfect' trading strategies of other traders. Nevertheless, they're not completely useless or unusable. Especially use them to get inspired. To see how others have developed their strategy and subsequently implement it in practice. Learn from their successes and mistakes. And use them all in your own trading strategy.

Trial and error. Put something on paper, start it, adjust it, test it, adjust it again, keep optimizing and perfecting it. That's how you'll come to the right trading strategy which suits you.

Advantages and disadvantages of working with trading strategies
Where we normally like to opt for a summing up of a number of pros and cons via several bullet points, today we'll keep it short and simple. Of course, there are advantages to trading strategies, otherwise we would never have started writing this book, but there are also disadvantages. We'll briefly summarize them for you.

Advantages
The biggest advantage of trading strategies is of course their structure. You know when you have to do something, why you're doing it and what's in store for you. It gives you focus and a direction. It ensures that your rational brain does the thinking instead of your emotions. In addition, with a trading log you build up a history.

You have a foundation in which you keep track of which trades have turned out to be successful for you, or not. And such a document is worth gold to fall back on at times when you still have doubts.

Disadvantages
Coming up with and maintaining a trading strategy takes quite some time.

Apart from that it could happen - certainly in the beginning - that you are confronted with a phase which we call "consciously incompetent". In this phase you'll actually find out how much there is still what you don't know.

But rest assured, this phase too will pass (soon enough). And based on new experiences you'll be able to fine tune your own crypto trading strategy and make it even better.

Cryptocurrency investment strategies

A good strategy to apply for holding Bitcoin or other cryptocurrencies is to only invest money that you do not need on the short term. Bitcoin for example, in its current state is still extremely volatile, and if you follow its course closely, and expecting only growth, you might be in for an emotional rollercoaster.

These are 5 steps for a successful Crypto Investment Strategy

Step 1: Decide how much money you want to invest

The first step to a successful cryptocurrency investment is always to determine the investment amount. Only when you know how much you want to invest in cryptocurrency, you can start developing an appropriate strategy for this. For example, if you only want to invest a small amount, then it may pay to choose the somewhat cheaper altcoins that you have done enough research on. It is crucial to understand what value the coin has within the financial system.

If you have more budget, then investing in Bitcoins, for example, could be an option. Therefore, always determine the investment amount in advance and make sure you don't deviate from it later on. It can be very tempting to invest more and more savings in cryptocurrency.

Although in some cases this can be smart (for example when you don't need the savings and you see nice investment opportunities), it is still important to keep sufficient savings in normal currency. This way, in case of an emergency, you don't have to immediately start selling cryptocurrency to be able to finance necessary (unexpected) expenses.

Step 2: Determine your appropriate investment strategy

Within investing in cryptocurrency, there are many different strategies imaginable. For example, you can choose to invest in the long term or in the short term. Which strategy suits you best depends entirely on your personal situation. Possible factors that may influence the strategy choice are, for example, how long you want to invest the money, how much time you want to invest yourself (daily or weekly) in your cryptocurrency and how much knowledge you already have about crypto coins.

There are generally two strategies you can follow when investing in cryptocurrency. The first strategy is to hold coins for a longer period of time in order to maximize profits. The second strategy is so-called day trading, where you buy crypto coins with the aim of selling them again in the short term.

There are generally two strategies you can follow when investing in cryptocurrency. The first strategy is to hold coins for a longer period of time in order to maximize profits. (long-term investment) The second strategy is so-called day trading, where you buy crypto coins with the aim of selling them again in the short term.

Set your goals

Trading stocks or cryptocurrencies is a big game between "Bulls" (buyers) and "Bears" (sellers). One group is betting that the price will go down while at the same time the other group is betting that the price will go up. Within Crypto Trading, you can roughly set two goals:

1. **Collecting more Bitcoin:** By trading Altcoins against Bitcoins, you ensure that you get more and more Bitcoin in your possession. People who choose this option trust that Bitcoin is going to become much more valuable in the long run, so they want to set as much Bitcoin as possible.
2. **Collecting more Fiat currencies (such as Euros, Dollars and more):** By trading Bitcoin or Altcoins against Euros, for example, you can ensure that you own more and more Fiat. This group of people use Bitcoin like any other tradable unit. So, they do not believe in the underlying value, but mainly find the volatility of the coin interesting.

Long term or Short Term?

The basics of trading and investing are easy: Buy cryptocurrencies when your price is low and sell them when the price is high. This is also called "long" in trading terms.
You can also do it exactly the other way around, sell your cryptocurrencies when the prices are high and buy back when the price has dropped. This is also called "Short" in trading terms.

Anyone who starts trading will basically always take a "long" position. You buy Crypto and sell it when the price is higher. Short positions are mainly used by experienced traders who also use leverage. However, we would advise against this for beginners, as it can also lead to you losing your money very quickly.

Step 3: Find the coins you want to invest in

Choosing interesting cryptocurrency, especially in the beginning, is probably one of the most difficult steps. When is it interesting to invest in a currency? When should I definitely not invest in a currency? If you knew the answers to these questions, you would be a millionaire within hours. Unfortunately, no one knows the answer to these questions 100% for sure, so in a way it always remains a gamble. but thanks to this book you have gained more insight into why Bitcoin can be a safe investment in the long run and how you can lose your money quickly by getting into a pump and dump scheme without prior knowledge.

So, by gaining enough knowledge about the coins you want to invest in, you can indeed make a good prediction. Of course, it's always smart to spread opportunities. Therefore, never invest in just one type of cryptocurrency, but spread your deposit at least over 2 to 3 different coins. Of course, it is also true that gaining knowledge remains an ongoing process. It is therefore not possible to say at a certain point that you have 'sufficient knowledge' of your coins and then not do any further research.

Step 4: The right moment

If you have been reading up on specific coins for a while, you probably already have an idea of the ideal purchase moment for yourself. To determine the ideal purchase moment, it is in any case wise to carefully analyze the prices of recent times. Often there is a clear pattern to be seen in the price developments of specific currencies. In addition, it is also important to determine the moment of sale.

When do you finally sell the coins again? The moment of sale is different for everyone. It depends entirely on the sales value with which you would be satisfied. Although the moment of sale is different for everyone, it is definitely wise to determine in advance at what price value you plan to sell your cryptocurrency. Of course, no one will ultimately force you to actually sell it for that value, but it does give you something to hold on to in the uncertain world of cryptocurrency.

Step 5: Ask for Help

Especially when you are just starting to invest in cryptocurrency, there are many things you won't know exactly yet. Although there is an enormous amount of knowledge to be found on the Internet, it can also definitely pay off to ask for help from the experts every now and then.
More and more financial advisors can provide excellent advice on investing in cryptocurrency. Of course, it is important to be critical when choosing a financial advisor. Costs are often high, but the right financial advisors who specialize in cryptocurrency cost nothing in practice. They provide far more profit than the cost of the advice you are spending.

At Stellar Moon Publishing, we work with a number of advisors who can provide you with appropriate advice to develop a profitable strategy for your crypto investments. Check out the contact options at the back of the book and let us know if you need help with your approach.

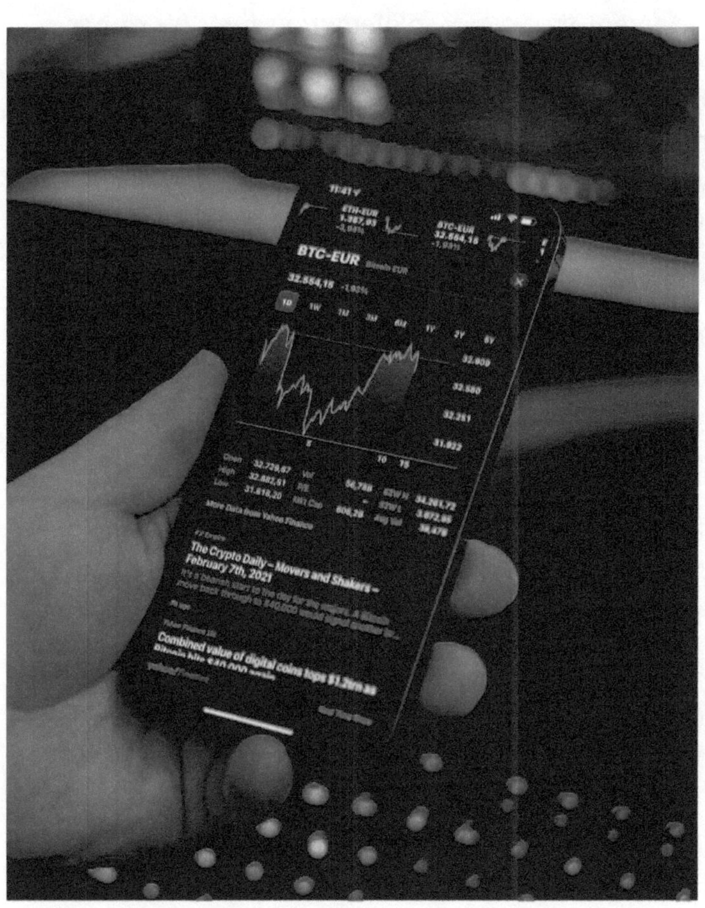

Essential tips for cryptocurrency success

The rules of safety are written in blood. This is a statement that every soldier who serves his or her country is familiar with. Although we are not discussing the risk to human life here, it is extremely inconvenient to lose your valuable Bitcoins due to mistakes made while you're trading and investing into crypto currencies.

Give each transaction a reason.

Only enter a **trading position**; *a price at which you want to sell or buy your coin.*

If you know why you want to sell or buy it and therefore have a clear strategy in mind.

Not all Crypto Traders can make a profit because this is a zero-sum game (where you make a profit, someone else on the other side loses).

Large coin holders (also called Whales in the crypto world) drive the alt & Bitcoin market - yes, the same "whales" responsible for buying and selling hundreds of Bitcoins at a time.

The whales patiently wait for unsuspecting small investors like us to make a trading mistake.

Even if you want to trade every day, it is sometimes better to do nothing than to jump into the rushing water and risk significant losses. Some days, you can make the most money by doing nothing at all!

Set clear goals and know when you need to stop

For each **trading position** you want to take, you must define a precise profit target level and, more importantly, a stop-loss level to limit losses.

Setting a stop-loss goal entails determining the maximum loss that can be accepted before closing the **trading position**.

Several factors must be considered when deciding on a stop loss level. The majority of traders fail because they "fall in love" with their position, meaning that the coins they hold, seem to go up in price, or they expect that it won't crash any lower, and they don't want to sell and take the profit/loss, or they fall in love with the cryptocurrency itself.

Meaning that no matter what, you choose to hold that coin for dear life. "I'm sure it will change, it will go higher, and I will exit this position with a minimal loss," they tell themselves. They allowed their ego to rule them.

In comparison to the traditional stock market, where 2-3% volatility is considered extreme, crypto transactions are much riskier: it is not uncommon for a cryptocoin to lose 80 percent of its value in a matter of hours. And you certainly don't want to be the one who is clinging to it!

Be aware of FOMO

Meet FOMO, which stands for "Fear of Missing Out." It's not fun to be on the outside looking in when a specific coin is pumped up like crazy with huge gains in just a few minutes.

That long green bar begs you to buy it, saying, 'You are the only one who isn't benefiting from this, so buy me!' At this point, you will also notice that many people and groups on Reddit, Telegram, and other platforms can only talk about this pump.

So, what are we to do? It's as simple as that: stay sober. True, the price may continue to rise, but keep in mind that the whales (mentioned above) are simply looking for small traders to sell their cryptocoins to.

Which they purchased at a lower cost. The price has risen, and it is clear that the coin is now in the hands of only a few smaller traders. Needless to say, when the coin is dumped in large quantities, the next step is usually a bright red price drop.

Risk Assessment

"Pigs grow fat; hogs are slaughtered." This quote tells the story of profit from the standpoint of success. To become a profitable Crypto trader, you should never seek out extremes. You seek out small profits that will add up to a large one.

Risk should be managed wisely throughout your portfolio. For example, you should never invest more than a small portion of your portfolio in a non-liquid (highly volatile) market. We will give those positions more leeway, and the stop and target levels will be set far away from the buy level.

Cryptocurrencies get traded for Bitcoin

This underlying asset causes market volatility: most altcoins are traded against Bitcoin rather than fiat currency (such as euros or dollars). Also see: What Is the Difference Between Cryptocurrency and Fiat Money?

Bitcoin is extremely volatile in comparison to almost any fiat currency, and this fact should be considered, especially when the price of Bitcoin fluctuates dramatically.

It was common in the early years for Bitcoin and altcoins to have an inverse correlation, which meant that when Bitcoin rose, altcoin prices fell relative to Bitcoin and vice versa. However, the correlation has become less clear since 2018. In any case, when Bitcoin is volatile, trading conditions become hard to determine.

Because we can't see far ahead during a volatile period, it's best to set close targets and stop-loss goals - or don't trade at all.

Use your alt-coins for trading

The majority of altcoins lose value over time. They can lose value gradually or rapidly.

However, the fact that the list of the top 20 altcoins has shifted so dramatically in recent years says a lot. Consider this when adding large amounts of altcoins to your portfolio for the medium and long term, and of course, choose them wisely.

If you are thinking about holding altcoins for the long term or building a crypto portfolio for the long term, pay close attention to the daily trading volume and conduct thorough fundamental analysis.

Altcoins with a thriving community have a good chance of surviving in the long run.

ICO, IEO, and token sales

Moving on to public ICOs (or IEOs, as they are now known in 2021): these are sales of crypto tokens. Many new projects choose to hold a crowd-sale, in which they provide investors with an early opportunity to purchase some of the project's tokens at a lower price.

The incentive for investors is that when the token hits the market, they will be able to profit handsomely. Many successful token sales have occurred in recent years, with ROIs of 10x not uncommon.

The Augur ICO, for example, provided investors with a 15x return. So, what's the catch? Not all of these projects return a profit to their backers. Many sales turned out to be total rip-offs. They were not only not traded at all, but some projects vanished with the money, never to be seen or heard from again.

So how do you know if you should invest in a particular token sale?

The amount of money that the project wishes to raise is an important consideration. A project that raises too little money will most likely be unable to develop a working product, whereas a project that raises too much money will likely not have enough investors to purchase the tokens on the market. The most crucial aspect is risk management. Never put all of your eggs in one basket, and avoid putting too much of your portfolio into a single IEO or ICO. They are classified as high risk.

Commissions

Performing multiple trades requires the payment of a higher commission. It is always better and less expensive for a market maker to place a new order in the order book rather than buy from the order book at a trading platform.

Don't create pressure

Start trading only when you have the best conditions to make the best decisions, and always know when and how to stop trading if necessary. Trading begins with a well-thought-out strategy! If you are under a lot of pressure, it will affect your decision-making ability. As a result, never rush.

Set targets and sale-orders

Set your goals by placing sell orders. You never know when a whale will pump up a coin in order to buy up the stock in the order book (and pay a lower price on the sale-order creator' side).

Buy the rumor, sell the news

When major news broadcasts publish news, this is usually the right time to sell the coin and not buying it!

Don't forget Murphy's Law

You made a profitable trade, but as is customary, the price skyrockets right after you sell. Don't give in to the temptation to change jobs. In other words, don't succumb to **FOMO** (Fear of Missing Out). You'll be fine as long as there are profits.

Don't let your ego rule your investments

The goal is to obtain PROFIT. Don't squander resources (time and money) attempting to demonstrate that you should have taken this or that position. Keep in mind that no trader only enters winning positions. The general rule is that the number of winning trades must exceed the number of lost trades.

Buy when the prices are low

Bear markets are sometimes the best times to make a profit, if coin is going down, that could mean it's the best time to buy in and make a profit over time. But make sure your plan is solid for the near future and you have some idea as to why the price drop is only temporary.

Buyers versus sellers

Consider the following hypothetical company. People who believe in the company purchase as many shares as they can at the $10 price.

However, in order to do so, there must also be people willing to sell their shares at this price. As a result, these people are skeptical that the price will rise. They would not sell if they thought it would! If a shareholder wishes to sell his shares, he is free to set his own price.

Assume someone lists his shares for sale at $12 each, and others want to buy at $10. In that case, both parties can agree on a price of $11 and meet in the middle. After the first trading day, the price of our donut shop is $11 per share. In many ways, this reflects how the market perceives our company.

This principle applies to cryptocurrencies in a similar way.

If you are a wise investor, you understand that you cannot learn everything simply by looking at the current price. Using historical data, you can estimate market sentiment. Is the current price too high or too low? What was the cost at the start of the day last year? Was there a price drop last quarter?

Pump and dump schemes

It's never a good idea to mindlessly follow a hype of a random coin, just because people claim to have made huge profits over night.

This generally indicates towards a "classic" pump and dump scheme, meaning that in order to make massive profit with a crypto coin, use the influence of news, crypto blogs, youtubers and other influencers, social media platforms such as Reddit and Facebook to hype up the price of a seemingly random coin.

The general idea of this is to buy in early and dump the amount of coins bought as the price rises a 1000-fold.

It's easy to recognize this pattern as the claims are usually in a trend as follows:

Random shitcoin launch price is $ 0.000001 with the claim that if this coin will climb to $ 0.001, you would make around 1000x profit.

These claims about random coins that are about to burst are all over the internet; Tiktok, Instagram, Facebook and Reddit are swarming with paid and unpaid advertisements regarding pump and dump schemes.

All of this simply means, whoever is in on it, can get massive profits as long as they get enough people to buy into the hype.

Influencers get paid to push this information.

It can pay up to $ 25,000 per post if you're an influencer willing to promote one of these schemes. Because if you build up a decent number of followers, there is a greater possibility that people will buy into whatever you have to tell them.

And as a content consumer, and someone who is looking to buy into the next hype, critical thinking is your best asset.

Dogecoin

The prime example of a pump and dump with social media influence, is what Elon Musk did with Dogecoin and Bitcoin, a couple of tweets and mentions about both coins, and as you probably saw in recent news, the price of Bitcoin and Dogecoin rises, and he bought in, especially into Bitcoin, before he started the rumor, he probably made a billion in profits from simply mentioning it in a tweet, same as he recently caused a crash in the Bitcoin price.

Elon Musk is a smart man in that regard, follow his investment strategy, where he buys up a massive amount of Bitcoin, claiming that his company Tesla, will now accept Bitcoin payments for the cars and drives up the price by a massive margin, an all-time high of over $60,000.

And not much later, Elon Musk drops a bomb, telling the internet that Bitcoin mining is terrible for the environment, meaning he sold out at the high price point, watched the market crash, and creating a new entry point for people to buy in.

He started to tweet about Dogecoin in early April, with the starting price around $0.05, and on 16th April, the price hit an all-time high of $0.39.

A short dip followed, the coin dropped back to $0.19 on April 23rd and after that it continued to rise back up towards a new high of $0.71 on May 5th, followed by another drop with the current price at $0.50.

There is not too much to say about the future of Dogecoin as it feels like some kind of joke. Elon Musk has proven himself in the past to be a big fan of internet culture, and have a currency such as Dogecoin, rule the financial market is nothing more than an elaborate joke.

So, if you feel lucky, you could buy in on Dogecoin and take the gamble that will double in price in the near future, but any success is entirely based on luck with a coin that has its price based on speculation. So, in essence investing in certain cryptocurrency is a bit of a gamble.

A good rule thumb if you're willing to gamble with pump and dump schemes is to buy in when the rumors start and start selling when it hits the mainstream news.

Since the price will quickly rise whenever a trending coin hits the mainstream news channels, it also means that a lot of people that bought in early, use this moment to cash out, sell the coin and get the profit, causing an almost immediate price drop when a large number of coins get sold on any of the markets.

Meaning that if you don't have solid information on when this dump will happen, you're bound to lose your stake, if you're late. Since cryptocurrencies are decentralized, they're basically impossible to regulate as long as the information gets out and trending.

Intrinsic value of cryptocurrency

Don't buy into new or relatively unknown coins as a long-term investment if they don't show any intrinsic value.

So, a solid piece of advice would be to know what you buy into, do you know if it is a so-called "shitcoin", a marketing scam that people use to drive up the price, or if the coin has real application value.

For example, Ripple (XRP) aims to become the next global payments network for financial institutions. If you follow the news around Ripple, it is a bit easier to predict what the price will do, right now they have a 40% stake in Asia's cross-border payments system and they work hard to solidify their future as a financial instrument.

Right now, creating a new coin takes about 5 minutes if you want to create a pump a dump scheme. Next up will be marketing, make sure people get know that your coin will be the next one that makes them rich and gain interest on the internet.

This coin has to be coin that doesn't need proof of work like Bitcoin does as explained in the chapter "**The Intrinsic Value of Bitcoin**".

So, if you want to start a coin yourself, make a copy of an existing coin that requires no effort to trade and start up, you could probably find a tutorial for setting this up on YouTube.

Call the new coin anything that with keywords such as safe, or going to the moon, such as the infamous Safemoon, claim that it's going to burst, and make sure as many people as possible need to hold on to that coin because it will make them rich. Preferably implementing a hefty fee if they want to sell it.

Publish a white paper about your coin; a white paper is an explanation of how the coin works, how to buy it and other vital information to get the interest of investors.

For a pump and dump scheme, this would ideally be a paper that claims some kind of transaction fee that gets paid out to the coin holders. The idea behind this transaction fee that pays out to the other coin holders is to create a sense safety for the potential investors.

If a new person buys some coins and they get their friends to buy some coins, everyone seems to profit from such a system. They want to create an illusion that if you get as many people as possible to buy that coin, everyone gets rich.

However, one crucial part that would make that possible is that the coin needs intrinsic value. If you need to buy in and keep the coin in order to gain value, it will be discouraging to sell them for dollars as in essence the price would drop.

109

And simply put, it's a dead system if the value has to come from people that have to buy in. That system only indicates, that once, enough people have bought in, the owners and large coin holders can sell out, make the value of that coin drop while other the people that are not in on the moment of selling out take a loss.

To put it into an example;

If person A buys 10 coins and you have a 10% transaction fee, 1 coin of these coins get divided over the other coin holders, so if there are 10 coin holders at this point, all of them would get 0.1 coin from that transaction.

Many of the scam coins that get promoted right now, they boast a similar type of system as explained the example, promising they will explode in value if enough people buy and everyone gets a share when someone buys in.

If you paid attention and read between the lines, you would have made the conclusion that this is the cryptocurrency equivalent of a pyramid scheme.

Safemoon and Shiba Inu: scam projects?

For those of us who have been following the crypto market for a while, we know that the bull run of 2017 and 2018 was accompanied by a slew of coins that were not only as volatile as Bitcoin, but also as volatile as the day Bitcoin crashed.

These scam projects, or shitcoins as some call them, give crypto a bad reputation, but it appears to be a good part of the industry as new technology. With all of the hype surrounding Bitcoin and Ether, we must keep in mind that a variety of smaller coins will also rise in value.

 As we explained previously, pump and dump schemes such as the infamous Safemoon, are basically the cryptocurrency equivalent of a pyramid scheme.

With the rapid rise of the Shiba coin, many people are wondering if a crash is imminent. As Binance announced earlier recently, the top #1, #2 and #5 wallets contain 50.5%, 7.0% and 3.0% of the total supply respectively, which would normally be extremely worrying, but in this case it's an even stranger story.

The developers at Shiba Inu sent 50% of their tokens to Ether founder Vitalik Buterin at launch.

We are a bit positive about the Shiba coin at the moment but it seems that because of the false sense of security, a situation is created with a low threshold to risk your money.

We predict that this coin will also be very volatile and will probably see a future as one of thousands of pump and dump projects.

Binance has also listed SHIB in their Inovation Zone, making it possible to buy Shiba Inu through the exchange (which can only be done after filling out a questionnaire).

However, Safemoon currently has over 1.9 million users, but Binance refuses to listen to it. While the CEO Changpeng Zhao previously said that when a project has a large number of users, they will listen it. There are more Safemoon users than at Shiba, also Safemoon provided a record number of transactions on the Binance Smart Chain.

The intrinsic value of bitcoin

Bitcoin has intrinsic value in its transaction. A Bitcoin transaction is a calculation, and doing that calculation gets a reward, a block, a Bitcoin, hence why it's called the blockchain. Since each Bitcoin transaction is a calculation that consists of every other calculation (consisting of previous transactions) leading up to the transaction.

So, since Bitcoin has been in use since 2009, these countless transactions have led to the point where it takes an immense amount of calculation power to complete a transaction. Doing these calculations is called mining, and it's a business where Bitcoin mining requires more electricity that a small country at this point.

In order to have the Bitcoin crash completely, people would have to stop trading it at a point in time where one transaction would cost too much to calculate it. Hence this principle ensures the long-term future of Bitcoin as long as people use it to trade.

Also, Bitcoin has been the fundamental currency of the black market because the owners of Bitcoin cannot be tracked through personal account details like having a bank account, thus Bitcoin can be used to buy anything outside of the law.

There is no bank or financial institution holding account details and personal information about Bitcoin owners. And if you want to keep your privacy with the amount of

Bitcoin you own, it is advised to keep it in a physical wallet such as the Trezor One.

So, in order to keep your transactions as off-grid as possible, make sure to use an anonymous route of buying your Bitcoin, and keep them off trading platforms that require personal details in order to use them.

Bitcoin trading privacy

Trading platforms for Bitcoin might require access to personal details in order to use that platform, especially since the certain governments want to track these transactions.

The platform Binance is under investigation right now for tax fraud and money laundering by the U.S. government, purely because the U.S. government want to track who is trading and who owns what on these platforms.

They even offered platforms to pay for personal details, and even though many crypto trading platforms claim to have perfect customer privacy, it wouldn't be the first time, they sold personal data to third parties. There are even some rumors that certain platforms sell out to the government, but nothing can be said for sure.

Bitcoin was built to decentralize value. As far as the past can teach us, money rules the world, and if you control large sums of money, you have nearly infinite power.

Another rule is also true, that money indefinitely corrupts, money has been the cause of greed, egoism and poverty all around the world and it's in the hands of a very small percentage of people.

Bitcoin can be used to destabilize the global store of value if enough people buy into it. Classic banking is built on inflation in the current economic system and if enough money flows into the crypto currency market, it will destabilize the inflation of regular money.

Banks use the money that people store to invest in whatever they deem to be profitable; they also used a good part of that value to create loans such as mortgages.
But at this point they have to keep printing out money to keep the system running, because more loans means less actual value of money. And if you put the value next to the current global flow of money, it's a giant bubble of credit bound to burst.

Why bitcoin is a solid long-term investment

This bubble of credit portrays why Bitcoin is such a solid investment for the long-term future. With the total trading value of Bitcoin in dollars right now, the entire market of Bitcoin is valued at a staggering $846,019,261,238.40, or shortly said, 846 billion dollars.

So, Bitcoin has reached a value of almost 1 trillion dollars, and it's coming close to overtake the dollar, which has around 1.2 trillion dollars worldwide.

To put the crypto market in perspective, the total market capitalization is valued at 2.2 trillion dollars.

Consider that Bitcoin mining will become exponentially more difficult, requiring more processing power and more electricity over time as long as Bitcoin is used. Another important fact for the value of Bitcoin is that the amount of Bitcoin is finite, meaning that at some point in time the last Bitcoin will be mined, and it's estimated right now that it will take more than a 100 years.

This means that the price of Bitcoin is nowhere near the price that it will be in 20 or more years and with the current rate of inflation, it's an extremely desirable store of value for the long term.

It's a fact that the dollar will inflate more, it seems that it has to come to a crash at some point since at some point it will simply make the prices unreasonably high, rendering the dollar more worthless of the course of time.

You can see proof of this in the prices of crude materials such as wood right now. These prices are sky-high, and they are slowly starting to destabilize the housing market.
The cause of this is in the fact that Donald Trump put a massive increase on import tariffs on wood from China in 2020, creating a situation where the U.S. buys up all the wood from Europe, driving up the price immensely.

This makes that renovation, new housing and other projects that require large amounts of wood are becoming much more expensive, even so that it influences prices on the real estate market right now.

Houses have been more expensive than ever in Europe to the point where it starting to cause problems in other markets.

This means banks have to give out a much large mortgage for a smaller house than 10 years which will only contribute to enlarging the credit bubble and its effect in every aspect of the economy.

Besides that, due to a multitude of complex financial problems, there is an inflation coming where bitcoin can be the solution to keeping the value of your capital healthy.

The current chip shortage

The biggest contributor to the store of value in Bitcoin is the chip shortage, Bitcoin is one of the driving factors of chips becoming more valuable and because of the higher demand it leads to an inflated price and shortage.

One of the speculations is that Elon Musk caused the crash because the chip shortage is also affecting the production of Tesla cars. So, disrupting the market price of Bitcoin, disrupts the market for Bitcoin mining equipment, this could potentially create a bit of space in the chip market.

A much-needed space for other manufacturers that really in one way or the other on chips and semi-conductors.

But the certainty remains that Bitcoin mining difficulty will increase as long as Bitcoin trading exists, demanding more from the chip market, and boosting prices for the equipment needed for Bitcoin mining.

Quantum computing will not have impact on Bitcoin mining

Simply put recent studies, done by Louis Tessler and Tim Byrnes, have shown that quantum computing cannot do Bitcoin mining more efficiently than current ways of Bitcoin mining. Hence, the proof of work from Bitcoin mining has a very stable future in the current computing environment without any threats that would make the proof of work in Bitcoin mining obsolete.

So, in conclusion, and taking in account all these different factors, it can be a very smart move for growing a long-term capital to invest a monthly amount of money in Bitcoin, that you would normally save on regular bank.

Sichuan Shutdown Order

Hash percentages from some of China's largest Bitcoin mining pools have fallen to 37% after Sichuan ordered energy companies to stop supplying power to mining companies in the province.

News of the cease-and-desist order broke yesterday after a meeting between the country's Science and Technology Bureau and Sichuan Ya'an Energy Bureau. Power companies were given until early Sunday, June 20 (Beijing time) to turn off the power.

Chinese mining pools are an integral cog in the global crypto-ecosystem, and many of the miners in these pools draw from Sichuan's abundant hydropower. Mining pools are cryptocurrency mining collectives that share their computing power to mine cryptocurrency

The cease-and-desist order issued to power companies identified 26 mining pools in Sichuan province.

"Molly," head of marketing at Chinese blockchain company Hashkey Hub, tweeted that the hash rate "already dropped significantly" after the Sichuan government announced it would cut off power to Bitcoin mining companies.

Hashrates for mining pools are: in free fall. Since Molly's tweet, some mining pool hashrates have dipped further. Mining hashrates on the best mining farm AntPool have dropped by 27.53%, while BTC.com's hashrate has dropped by 18.34% and Huobi.pool has dropped by 36.79%.

China has cracked down on cryptocurrencies in recent months. It has had a knock-on effect on the global price of crypto. Bitcoin's worst crash in 12 years got worse last month when payment associations repeated support for a 2017 ban on crypto transactions.

The state's next target was mining operations. On June 9, Xinjiang province ordered several crypto miners shut down. In the notice, Xinjiang cited "Measures for the Examination of Energy Conservation of Fixed Asset Investment Projects" - a bit of regulation first issued in 2016.

The country's massive crackdown on currencies like Bitcoin and Ethereum, which are difficult to regulate, sets the stage for the state's central bank-backed currency: the digital yuan. China is currently testing the currency, which as of yesterday can be converted into fiat for over $XNUMX million 3,000 ATMs in Beijing.

Given China's profound influence on cryptomining and market value, today's drop could seriously reshape the Bitcoin mining industry as we know it.

Conclusion

You should have a good idea of how to conduct your own risk assessment when it comes to investing in cryptocurrencies by now. And, before you begin, make sure you have a plan, do your research, and are eager to learn the value of the coin you wish to invest in.

One of the most important rules of investing is to educate yourself on the hype before you begin. Instead of paying for someone else's profit with the next pump and dump scheme, make sure your investment is calculated.

And, if you want to make huge profits with day trading, making real money from the previously mentioned pump and dump schemes, make sure you get a reliable source of information. There are numerous free and paid investment groups that can provide you with solid insights on coins with high short-term trading potential.

If you like the sound of a high risk, high reward approach to cryptocurrencies, Binance Futures trading could be an option.

Let us know what you think of the book, and if it has proven to be useful, please leave us a review so that others can benefit as well.

Thank you for reading our book, and good luck with your future investments!

Your FREE book

If you want to make a profitable start in the world of cryptocurrency, make sure to download our free bonus with **12 extremely valuable tips for beginners!**

With this book and these tips, you're guaranteed to make a great start with your future investments!

Sign up here to get instant access and kickstart your crypto success:

https://campsite.bio/stellarmoonpublishing

Our books

Check out our other book to learn more about NFTs, NFT trading and selling, how to make profit and essential tips and strategies for a fail-proof start in the NFT universe.

Join the exclusive Stellar Moon Publishing Circle, you'll get instant access to **12 Extremely Valuable Crypto Tips**!

Besides that, you'll also get instant access to our mailing list with updates from our experts every week!

Sign up here today:

https://campsite.bio/stellarmoonpublishing

Our Crypto Expert Trading Course

Are you looking for a new way to invest?

Are you looking to make some money?

Interested in investing but do not know where to start?

Do you want to start your crypto trading with the knowledge of reputable experts in finance and investment?

The crypto Expert Trading Course is the most comprehensive course on trading and investing with cryptocurrencies. You will learn how to trade in just a few minutes per day. We

126

teach you everything from technical analysis, risk management, and much more.

Our goal is to help you become a successful trader so that your financial future can be secure.

Investing has never been easier with our step-by-step blueprint that teaches beginners how to trade like an expert – with the potential of making huge profits!

The best part about this course is taught by experts. So, what are you waiting for? Start today!

For more information, visit this link:

https://payhip.com/b/ork8N

www.ingramcontent.com/pod-product-compliance
Lightning Source LLC
Chambersburg PA
CBHW020724160726
47993CB00006B/2335